# NOTE FROM THE PUBLISHER

Welcome back! We had an exciting spring on Ibbetson Street. The Endicott College/Ibbetson Street Press Visiting Author Series hosted a number of fine poets and writers this season, including Michael Gerhard Martin, X. J. Kennedy, and Diana Der-Hovanessian. The Endicott College/Ibbetson Street Press Young Poet Series released another new poetry collection by a talented undergraduate, Paige Shippie, entitled: *Human Cycles*.

In this issue of *Ibbetson Street* you will experience poetry by such fine poets as Jared Smith, Brendan Galvin, Jennifer Barber, Kathleen Spivack, Marge Piercy, Linda Conte, and many more. We are very pleased that Melissa Shook, a retired Professor of Photography at the University of Massachusetts Boston, and a nationally and internationally exhibited photographer, has a self-portrait gracing our front page, and an alluring sketch adorning our back. Shook wrote us that:

> In December of 1972, I started a series of daily self-portraits, a conceptual piece that I wanted to continue for a year. The idea was to record whether I forgot the project—in a sense forgot myself—so the days when I took no image are as interesting to me as the ones when I did. I had so little sense of self, though the photographs show a woman in her early thirties. Quite by accident, the photographs I'd been taking of my daughter were discovered; they and part of the self-portraits were published in the Camera 35 Annual in 1974; then some were purchased by the Museum of Modern Art and subsequently became part of two group shows, the last one in 2010. The published work led to my being hired to teach in the Creature Photography Department at MIT, my first full-time teaching job, which lasted three years. That's how I left New York, and I don't know why I could never get back.

As always, we thank Endicott College for its continued support. We also thank our poetry editor Harris Gardner, managing editor Lawrence Kessenich, and designer Steve Glines for putting this issue together. See you again in November!

—Doug Holder, Ibbetson Street Press, May, 2015

Ibbetson Street Press
25 School St.
Somerville, MA 02143

Publisher: Doug Holder
Managing Editors: Lawrence Kessenich, Rene Schwiesow
Poetry Editor: Harris Gardner
Consulting Editors: Robert K. Johnson, Dianne Robitaille, Emily Pineau
Art Consultant: Richard Wilhelm
Design: Steve Glines
Website Manager: Steve Glines
Front cover photograph and back cover art: Melissa Shook

Boston Area Small Press and Poetry Scene http://dougholder.blogspot.com
Doug Holder's CV: http://dougholderresume.blogspot.com
Ibbetson Street Press http://ibbetsonpress.com
ISCS PRESS http://www.iscspress.com
Ibbetson Street Press Online Bookstore http://www.tinyurl.com/3x6rgv3

The Ibbetson Street Press is supported by and formally affiliated with Endicott College, Beverly, Massachusetts. http://www.endicott.edu

No simultaneous submissions; no poems previously published in print or online. All submissions must be sent by email only to tapestryofvoices@yahoo.com—as an attachment or pasted into the body of the email.

# CONTENTS

## SIGNALS

If she asks
you up, say yes.

Coffee?  Tea?  A drink?
Say tea.  Follow

shyly into the kitchen.
Wait.

Stroke the countertop.
If the cups

have saucers, ask
after her mother.

Carry them
reverently as candles to the table.

If there is no pot,
only a copper kettle, reminisce

about the dented ones
of your childhood.

Sit close.
Does the pot

remind you of an amphora?
Laugh.  Quote Keats.

If it has bamboo handles,
listen; tilt

your face toward her.
Savor the steam, the warmth,

her voice.  If the pot
is hand-thrown, heavy

as a prehistoric figure;
if the spout reminds you

of breasts, grow silent.  Murmur
Yes, yes, yes.

*—Jessie Brown*

## POEM FOR MY FIRST LOVE

Seven months
into my 77th birthday
I slip back in time

I'm driving down highway one
where California's fertile hills
wink at me

giant trees and seashore
merge as one
cloudbanks ride the horizon
like Geronimo rode the plains
in search of the last buffalo

sweet mangos
and watermelon wine
sweet as cotton candy
stuck to the roots of my tongue
fed my youth nourished my spirit
the poem the language in my soul
your body indented against mine
hot as an iron
pressed to a garment

a youthful hunger that
knew no bounds
feasted like a condemned man
devouring his last meal
the way Eskimos used to swallow
the tears of the dying
to keep the one gone
with them

*—A.D. Winans*

**"In Juno, They Got Northern Lights, But Betelgeuse and Cassiopeia Come Every Summer to Franklin Park."**

July creek nights, lightning bugs star sycamores
for Nikki's hot pink brassiere strap ten o'clock showing
and Grady's Ready-lite dynamite—the original firecrackers,
eyes dusted with lemon yellow tailpipe reflections
while 2,000 miles away a young New Zealander points to the Aurora
Borealis, asks his father, "How did all the rainbows get drunk?"
The ex-pat Cracker, who still has feelings for his first wife,
lifts the product of their union onto his shoulders, dances
his son in a shamrock pattern, answers, "On the rye whiskey
lemonade of Agenbite's Inwit, my sweet chaser!"

—*Amy Wright*


## WHEN PIGS FLY

They lack the aerodynamics of their avian neighbors,
the eagle, or even the pigeon,
but instead have the simplicity and grace of the
soap bubble or the circus balloon.

On summer nights, the patient and sharp-sighted may pick out
a lonely silhouette as it passes by the pearl of the moon.
This filthy little poet, so at peace with the earth that
she rolls herself around in—covers herself in it,
it is her heart that is so heavy.

For ten-thousand years she has been
mankind's cruel punch-line: little pig, little pig.
Her nourishment has been his filth, his bile, his abuse.
She is never mentioned with the nobility of the horse,
the wisdom of the owl, or the camaraderie of the dog.

So on a summer night, when she sees the moon
sparkling in her water trough, and her small mouth
can curl up at her own reflection,
then she can lay her leaden heart down,
kick her delicate hooves from the earth, and rise.
Rise over the chimneys, over the weather-vanes,
over the petty barnyards of her ancestors.
Rise into great, pink clouds of clarity, peace, and gladness.

—*Thomas Libby*

*Listening to the traps of our own unworthiness .....*
*Listening to the music of our own salvation ... ... ......*


### An angel


caught up in a whirlwind
of wires    began to struggle
to undo  his windings from
the spiral    and tried
and tried    and tried again
he could not regain his freedom
          without breaking one of his wings

stayed there a long time
in awe shouted for help
birds passed by     did not hear anything
other angels stopped        smiled at him
he looked at them and raised his eyebrows
waited for them to save him
thinking they understood
he needed to be helped

he was trapped
no more flying over the earth:
the spacious sky peace to his being
no more adventures    no running after other angels he adored
no more dreams curving the silenced winds and the singing clouds
his old forms vanished                his inner scars healed
he became only words        he became one with all

**he was he,   part of the flock**

—*Beatriz Alba Del Rio*

## EPIPHANY

    After *Epiphany* by Max Ernst

No one told us the shepherds' names (the dishonored, the thieves). And no one knows what star the Magi followed (which king brought Frankincense, which brought myrrh, or how many kings there really were). Who knows what they thought of the cobbled sky or, if, after finally seeing, their bodies went into the distance without them—sheep like clouds on far-off fields.

Deep inside the wind's white dream, a river stills. There's more snow pending … that coming and coming again … and so many things to purposely forget. In winter, the world is undone—its light spent. What is here is simply here, where we are—where we've been headed all along. How many ways do we say *change?*

                                                *—Adele Kenny*


## EVENING AS FOOTNOTE (a Haibun)

Evening as footnote after the long day's rain. A scrap of curtain moves in and out of the window. My friend Joe writes, *A little drooping death never hurt a poor boy.* Joe grew up poor. We both did—you get used to such things, things that equal loss. Somehow, though, you never adjust to the way love comes and goes, how what you're left with is never exactly what you need.

       nightfall:
       the corners of the room
       disappear first

                                                  *—Adele Kenny*

## THE DREAMER

We sat in my mother's chairs,
my sister and I,
looking out the wide front window,
watching the bay, seeing the same view
my mother had seen every day.

As the sun set, one building across
the bay always burned gold for
a minute before the flame went out.

The room was abstract, almost empty.
We looked like figures in an
Edward Hopper painting,
not moving, paused between actions,
anticipating the next moment.

From an owls-eye view in the rafters
at the back of the room,
you could have seen this perspective:
bare floor, light from a low angle,
two armchairs, white, rounded,

each person's arms rendered
in a primary color,
outspread along the chair's' curves,
a dark head and a light one,
staring out a window as vast as a wall,
a frame for the scene beyond.

We talked a little, quiet and still.
We were learning not to expect
my mother
to come through the kitchen door
with a tray of things to eat,
drinks clinking with ice cubes.
We were awake, but my mother
was asleep and dreaming.

My mother dreams she is pushing open
the door with her tray, about to
call out to us in her musical voice,
"Look: that building in the city
is shining gold;"

She dreams she is putting one foot
forward into the room, preparing
to walk towards us.
But that's as far as she goes.

To her, time has stopped in that moment,
the moment she loves best—
when all is ripe with potential,
the tipping point when
wonderful things begin.

My sister and I didn't know
she was there in her dream,
paused at the entrance
before the action.
All three of us were waiting:

She was on one side and
we were on the other.
To us, my mother is only
a shadow, a whisper,
a remembered image to be
imagined but no longer experienced.
To her, we are real, and she
is about to enter the picture.

A viewer of the painting can see
the half-open door, a woman
striding forward with a tray in her hands.
The viewer can see two people
gazing out the window.
But the door is behind them;
the sisters do not see their mother.
She has not yet called out to them.

Across the bay, the building still glows
golden, silent.

—*Lucy Holstedt*

## AFTER FOURTEEN YEARS
*In memory of Daniel Patrick O'Connor*

You're here in the wild
grin of brown boulders
along the jewel-crusted coast of Maine.
You're here in the panting
of the dog by my side,
in the way that the wind blows
through an empty blue bottle
like a flute from the Andes
or the high lonesome sound
of the Appalachia we knew.
You're here in the quicksand
and the low groan of fog horns
in the sharp scent of pine needles
returning to earth. You're the breeze
in a coffee mug smiling improbably,
lying in wait on the path to the sea.
Walking this garden in the cool
of the evening, I find myself asking,
Where are you now? I know only this,
dear friend long departed:
You've poured out your life
into this luminous world.
There's nowhere now
you are not.

—*Alexander Levering Kern*

## RESURRECTION
*I found it nearly impossible
to look through the viewfinder.*
    –Zoriah, photojournalist

In each photo, we see
the clean measure of death:

a cane lies where a body stood;
a thumbless hand collects flies.

In one photo, a man's skull
blooms beneath the Anbar sun.

In another, a man points
to the ground, while blurry

soldiers sort the wreckage
along the photo's edge.

At its center, an old man
slouches in a plastic chair.

He looks asleep. No one touches him.
They hesitate, as if there's a chance

he'll wake, unwrap the blood-
stained scarf of gauze

bandaging his neck,
smooth his white *thawb*,

and leave the damaged chair
to walk, again, among them.

—*Adam M. Graaf*

## LAST PHOTO

The look on his face
isn't acceptance; isn't fear;
neither a need to be among
his gathered children
nor a desire to be alone.
It's more like disbelief
through which
the sharp intelligence
is showing, like light through glass,
unable to come to a stop.

*—Jennifer Barber*


## TIME LAPSE PHOTOGRAPHY

How tightly timed, the mystery of aging.
We lie down young, we wake up old.
Imagine faith, which is a mustard seed
sown in our brains and britches, hot to grow.
Arthritic twitches are a gift from God,
though atheists get them, too, no one knows how.
You've heard of faculties, those fascist boards
that rule our intellects? We mustn't lose them,
though frankly they can be such sassy bastards.
It rains today, I'm in my lean-to
poking the shadowed air with my savvy finger,
being "all there"—figuring the slate
of all I've done, of all I'd ever mean to.
Sane, mad, my mind is glad of both.
I have my faculties in mellow measure,
yet do without them sometimes, when it seems
there's something not quite sane that must be seen to.
A day like this, the rain, my snug redoubt,
I'm old enough to juggle mortal thoughts
but not what you would call decrepit, would you?
Sure as Christ rose, we're being photographed,
sequential frames the Reaper posts at random.
Old's the new young. Dead's the new old, I guess.
A dash of irony, a drop of gloom,
I'm only saying there are pictures taken.
The young, the old, they pose, they decompose.

*—Tomas O'Leary*

# JULY 4<sup>TH</sup>, LAKE GEORGE

The air cool and fresh, the lake's a dazzle of
whitecaps and gray-blue waves, the sun
breaking out in applause between a rhapsody
of wind-driven cumulus. Flags snap
on decks and boathouses and fly straight out
on the boats that skip up and down the lake.

I've put down the newspaper's infernal sadness,
and I'm enjoying a group of teenagers trying to tie
two of those rented pontoon boats together.
They're already half-drunk, laughing, happy
in their incompetency, a Marx Brothers' movie
of a rope thrown from one boat to the other.

In the foreground, a trio of kayaks, red, yellow,
and blue, and the glint of paddles making
figure eights in air and water. A backdrop
of mountains looks down like gods who have
seen it all a million times, but, stretched out
in the sun, are as yet too lazy to exert their whimsy.

In their shade, five seemingly still sailboats, give
the speedboats their speed; their distant sails tilt
white triangles into the wind as in a child's drawing.
The Minne-Ha-Ha steams down the far side
of the lake and the Lac du Saint-Sacrement huffs
and puffs up this side, each of them packed tight

with people reveling in the mindless freedom
of a perfect day off, waving to all of us on our docks,
as the two boats blow greetings to one another.
Everything shimmers in the sun, and I'm imagining
the whole scene as one of those Impressionist paintings,
a beach scene of people dressed in gay colors

and holding color-coordinated umbrellas, happy to be
exactly where they are, or so it always seems.
And since I'm looking again at the ongoing comedy
on those pontoon boats, I might as well prescribe
a dose of that teenage idea of freedom without obligation
for myself and forget about finding some meaning

I'd only force on this rapturous day anyhow—
I'll just sip my gin and tonic, and enjoy
my unpursued happiness on this freighted day.

*—Robert Cording*

## ADDING IT UP

The name's Time Bandit on the transom
of a trawler whose beam is too wide
for the lane. Getting down route 28
behind it will take awhile, but at least

the diesel blasts off the cab
and the shimmy of seaweed
like hula skirts on either
side of the hull are distractions.

What you hear this time of year
at the bar or next booth at the diner
is, "I'm a sixty-year-old captain
with an eighty-year-old hull."

Cod's high in the market, low on the docks,
and the mackerel have vanished.
Midwater trawlers suck the catch up
like an Electrolux.

Today the harbor's a gray heave,
the dunes so lapped with snow
the Arctic comes to mind. No crewman
would admit that Stellwagen Bank

puts something in the red corpuscles
when the moon rises and the only
life in the world is on that deck.

The Time Bandit's got civil serpents
boxing it in with permit banks and mesh sizes.
Seals and dogfish follow in its wake. Still,
it's on its way to the boatyard for
another overhaul.

Fish here not there, yesterday
but not next week. The crew's got leased
and traded quotas, catch shares, more like
brokers than fishermen. Remembering
how bread-and-butter nets could draw

a half ton of yellowtail with one pass,
no At-Sea Monitor on board to throw a fish-fit
over the by-catch, they're doing the math,
too old to stay in, too broke to get out.

—*Brendan Galvin*

## IN WINTER

I first met death in an alley
on a February morning,
crackling, frigid.

A cat
frozen stiff and stuck fast
to the icy ground,
its eye like a glass bead,
stared up at the Iowa sky.
I stared back.

My little brother
careened down the icy slope.
His sled flew over the retaining wall
at the bottom of the hill and crashed
in the street below.

A torrent of blood
spouted from a gash in his chin,
ran down the front of his snowsuit,
pooled in a crimson puddle
on the crystalline snow.

20 winters later,
he was dead.
But not from that.

—*Michael Gillan Maxwell*

## NIGHT VISITATIONS

By night the restless come, demand to be heard. They want to be seen to tell
their stories.
They wait on hard benches. The marble hall echoes, their words
reverberate.        A woman flees her past, invents a life
gives gifts to the child she was.


From deep in the drains
the midnight voice sings with a bang and rattle of the lost
who pull red wheeled lives.
Under the sign of the jukebox they dance
to music no one hears. Hearts break as they whirl
and a paralytic cries.
One o'clock. Insomniacs pace and a fool sleeps on the steps.

Here pranksters revel. Sounds crash, repel off towers
in a duet of metal on metal squeal and grind.

Silent in the night, lights flash red, green, yellow
into the room where a woman knits
(bit by bit the pattern comes together)
Tales of forgotten journeys:
of camel rides through sand
of a boy who washed his socks in his hat
as a homesick soldier called "Sui Sui" to the pigs across a far field.

By night moments hold, time is fluid, trembles on the edge. In the mirror
images repeat, slip back and forward
as voices tell and re-tell their stories
their words flow
weave snarled thoughts into semblance of sense.

—*Molly Mattfield Bennett*

## PORTRAIT OF THE ARTIST
## AS AN ARTIST

The crowded photograph sings
of everything hung on the wide wall:
a glistening torrent of
Moroccan metal finely wrought
into vases, baskets, frames
to fit the large mirrors—
and displayed in designs
intricate as dreams

        while, subtle
as a whisper, and dressed
in a black that blends
with the dark background encircling her,
her face anonymous
behind the mask of her camera,
is the photographer,
detectable only in one corner
of one mirror's reflection.

        —*Robert K. Johnson*

## FERNS

I pray for ferns in the garden,
hanging like many a verdant octopus
on slanting balconies of a house painted green,
*my* house in a recomposed Eden.
I pray for a month of Sundays—
holidays with God, sitting intimately
again on the emerald bench
of childhood near a mossy pool
where frogs frolicked indecently.
I pray that I will always pray,
always know that silence hears,
always perceive how divinity responds,
and grasp that there is no finality in death,
but an eternal accounting of gestures
whose consequences proliferate.

        —*Marilène Phipps-Kettlewell*

## LANGUAGES
*Mistranslations of languages
you've never heard.*
    *- Gloria Mindock*

We are proud to know a human tongue
or two, but are surrounded by languages
far richer. The inscrutable whisper

of grasses on the plains. Mute rocks,
which would tell tales of fire and water
if we pressed them to ear instead of underfoot.

The Morse code of stars, which we read
only at our most joyful or desperate,
when emotions burst open earthbound ears.

Who even understands the language of
his own heart, that confusing burble of messages
carried from it to the extremities?

Much less the language of another's heart.
Where is the Rosetta Stone for that?
Who will teach us to climb the Tower of
Babel and, this time, find our way?

        —*Lawrence Kessenich*

## WHY BEES HUM

The ancients say that Zeus so loved the bees
he made them golden like the sun,
imparting to each one
a ray of sacred fire, finely spun—
bright scarves in which they wouldn't freeze
when winter bared the trees.

Freed from the mortal fear of winter time,
whose threat the god had stooped to lift,
and grateful for the gift,
the bees spread out through autumn fields to drift
among the flowers, or cling and climb
and sip of the sublime

unhurried and unworried. Given heat,
they celebrate by making something sweet.

        —*Alfred Nicol*

## CHRISTINA'S WORLD

*Of course, she's an old cripple, for Pete's sake!*
—*Andrew Wyeth*

He saw her scuttle crabwise
across the field beyond the lawn.
Thin arms prop and propel; a bundle of sticks
dragging a kit bag on an exposed hillside—

but for the pink dress, the hip curve,
the compass needle of unruly hair
pointing to the cove beyond
the elliptical runway of the rutted road.

She wore down hard New England acres
with her passage from spinster farmhouse
to bachelor barn. It took an awareness
to lift her from the grass, to see her

for what she was. He learned this
from his father, would pass it on
to his son.  Once he saw one,
he found them everywhere.

Here in Maine, tides swap land and sea,
Aputamkon and selkie appear
 in hidden pockets along its craggy coastline.
To find them, you must first look away.

In the patient tempera hours models
let down their guard. He did everything
he could to keep them from singing
as he painted. The scuba girl, his wife

on that blueberry afternoon before the storm,
the sentinel dog a distraction—how could one
intrude and belong? He keeps their secrets,
reveals almost enough to satisfy as they shift

back and forth. Privilege granted in that moment
just before or after, perfect light
captures as they emerge.

—*Valerie Lawson*

**What didn't happen here**

Decades ago these streets were laid
in a grid pattern.  Even an occasional
fireplug stands hidden in tall grasses
that wave over it dropping tassels
of seeds on its faded metal.

Someone expected families to come
and settle in suburban tracthouses.
The trees were chopped down.  Now
second growth sumacs and birches,
willows and aspens have already

replaced the bushes that colonized
each neat square, ignoring property
lines, curbs, pushing up slabs
of pavement.  The subdivision is
hardly unoccupied.  I startled

a rabbit and suspect a nest's near.
A red fox sticks its pointy face
between two young maples, vanishes.
Chickadees, towhees, warblers. A feral
cat orange as milkweed flowers crouches.

I cannot help finding this an improvement
over a developer's dream.  A forest
is coming that requires no council's
approval. Like a stone wall found in deep
woods, our intrusion is almost erased.

—*Marge Piercy*

**THE SPEECHLESS JOY
OF SUMMER**

What we say must not
injure the silence
wrapped around trees

spider silk needs to
float in sunlight
totally free of mad whispers

I'd rather watch
a beetle crawl up my arm
than listen

to some people
talk rather see
nasturtiums curve

orange red yellow
clematis pronounce
spiral glories count

ten innocent earth stars
but interpretation
is a heavy chain

weighing down
the stem of a flower
better the speechless

joy of summer the sun
stretching days wide
over lilies and daisies

thick clumps of shaggy weeds
make bridges for bugs too
beautiful to cut down.

—*Nina Rubinstein Alonso*

## ABSTRACT LANDSCAPE

Performing her monthly breast self-exam
she moved her fingers in a circle
dutifully kneading into their soft reaches
pretending she wasn't touching

the pastures of pleasure
the rolling fields where babies
get their health and
reel on the grass drunk with love.

She found what she'd been looking
for – a pea? a pearl? bringing
behind it a towering tsunami wave
that broke the world.

Off to the side of the canvas
is the dark corner
the purple and ocher
where she squatted,

each bone screaming,
her wasted breasts still intact,
they were taken only
after her life was smashed and saved.

Enter the painting not thinking
of breast cancer, take a turn through
the colors, dianthus pink streaks
sending emerald tendrils into

cerulean sky.  As soon as
her rent torso had knitted back
she stood, like a prize fighter
dancing before the canvas, her brushes.

—*Laurie Soriano*

## COUNTING ON THE CURE-ALL

Put a raw steak on it or try
a cure all—soak a cotton ball

in apple cider vinegar then dab
the latest swelling circumference.

Rub black pepper or honey
massage vigorously, whatever

old wives tale you want to believe.
Manage to maintain something false;

a configuration—control bloom
and wane of the habitual bruises

patterns with familiar vicinity and rate
of recurrence. The shadow of the paddled

boar bristle brush, mark of brass buckle
four finger and thick thumb, spread wide-

open hand, measure the height
and width, outline eight by four inches.

That's about right for the average man's hand.
Pretty much all a child needs to know is the
fist

has a presumed speed — 20 to 30 mph.
It takes just eleven pounds per square inch

to choke an adult. A child, even less—
two fingers of whisky, two thumbs

above my brother's voice-box.
Encode the gathered data, find logic

in the face of horror, count down
the protracted seconds, array of shades

my older sibling's face turns colors—
a contusion turning red to mauve.

Count on Monday coming and count
on playing cool at school. Count

on brother popping his collar up—
Keep your mouth shut.

He's been blue just thirty seconds.
Don't count him out cold, not yet.

Count on some cure all, black pepper
or honey, last two fingers of whiskey

bottle, neck massage, thumbs working
counter clockwise, put a steak on it

moving contusions backwards
in time. He will wake. You can count

on it, count on the cure-all
count on Monday coming.

                    —*Teisha Dawn Twomey*


## LEAVING

Until this moment she has not understood that even her own street
sprawls like a prairie on early winter mornings.
That it hangs open as uninspired air, air un-exhaled, except by birds
that blur the naked trees when they merge on the horizon, and
that the yellow taxi waiting by the curb, its meter running,
could be a kind of Conestoga wagon.

Coming out the door,
carrying a single suitcase and her purse,
she who has never traveled anywhere and isn't traveling this time,
takes in the faces of her neighbors' houses. Nothing there.

She stops to watch the early morning shadows
spread like stains beside each solid thing, the way the wild flat
places on the range will run with cloud shapes dragged by wind.
Across the street, a single halogen in its metal hood on its pole
hums, in harmony with her ear's drumming.

She understands that when she gets to the Divide
all that has gone one way will reverse
because it has to, because she'll be on the other side.
No more the *Do Not Enter* she's stared at all her married life,
she's following a new sign.
The note on the kitchen table mentions that
but it does not say goodbye.

                    —*Miriam O'Neal*

## WE SAT EVERY NIGHT
### *For my grandmother*

We sat every night, watched the news
as Freedom Riders boarded buses
in your home state,
traveled to Montgomery, to Birmingham.

I was eleven:
*The government says colored people can vote, Nana,*
*why are whites against it?*

*People up North are always criticizing us southerners*
*but the colored are still treated*
*with more respect in southern states*
*than most anywhere else.*

Pictures of a scorched bus, people choking
by the side of the road. *Where is that 'anywhere else'?*
I wanted to be like the twelve-year-old white girl,
Janie Miller,
who filled five-gallon buckets with water,
carried them to the road
to help the Freedom Riders
when a crowd surrounded their bus
outside the city limits of Anniston and flaming rags
were thrown into the windows and they barely escaped.
I wanted to be brave. I wanted to do something.

I argued with you
as we watched pictures of inflamed white mobs,

*What about that?*

*Honey, these riots have not equaled the violence*
*that has taken place in many other places.*

*Where are those 'other places'?*

but my words
are leaves
swirling on your patio
as you rise to fix me another slice of pecan pie
the way I like it, warm,
with vanilla ice creams melting on top.

*—Lee Varon*

## IT IS NOT THE TRAIN

It is the men who cry,
the orphans who build boxcars.
It is the prisoners who roll
from cages to build wheels,
the slaves who carry iron
bars across earth for coins
or worse for paper patronage
as dust obscures the rails.

It is not the train that cries,
not the train carrying moonlight
down canyons of no name,
not the train with black boxes
opening to carry seeds of life
to let in the open air of the sea
to fill each box with amber
to move from one lover to another
shaking the earth with its passage
speaking only to the winds.

—*Jared Smith*


## BEHIND THE COUNTER

Faded generals in golf carts
seek routes to resurrection

Ghosts of July 4 at the counter
want tour books to heaven or hell

The elderly ask for the road
to their youth

The young seek detours
from the future

While behind the counter
the lost people

on earth take orders
plot trips to oblivion

—*Zvi A. Sesling*


## ON THE HILLS OF THE GOLAN— TWO WORLDS

A narrow road runs
below Mt. Hermon's alabaster hills—

to the east,
a column of sand-colored tanks
on maneuvers, crawls
like a rattlesnake,
silent, ready.

Pulled from their lives,
young men in dusty helmets,
almost invisible,
inch along
the chalk-white path

where heat burns
through cactus, in waves
of withering light.

To the west,
burgundy vineyards
glow in citrine sun,

lined up in long neat rows
of woody vines
and claret florets,

lush as they were
in the time of Moses,
when from the Valley of Eschol
came a cluster of grapes
so large, that it was borne
*between two upon a staff.* *

Hot light spreads,
like mist
across the Hula Valley.

where oranges hang,
in searing mountain sun,
so ripe
that they might burst.

—*Ruth C. Chad*

\* (Numbers 13:23)

## BLUEBERRIES

On the northern tip of Cape Ann,
on the ridge overlooking the quarry,
just off the wide gravel path
that leads to Halibut Point:

blueberries. Some dusky grey,
some so deep blue
they are almost purple,
almost black, small blueberries,

pert, dark pearls hanging among
unripe green pebbles.
These berries grew on this ridge
before Puritans, Pilgrims, Christians.

They lived their quick lives and deaths
with the blackbirds and cormorants.
Were they thicker then? Less
mercury in their roots? Were they

the same deep, dusky shades
that cover the hillside now,
raindrops of the night that approaches
across the unruly Atlantic?

Somewhere beyond the brush
and trees, the flat water
of the abandoned quarry
is swallowing the evening sky.

—*J.D. Scrimgeour*

## GOOD MORNING

Dreams last night were dark
and sad, though the morning sun
has dissolved them all.

Another day to greet
as it takes me by the hand
down a path that grows shorter
every year.  Hello, today!
What can I do to play with you?

I have no onerous responsibilities
I left them somewhere,
can't remember where.

The garbage must be taken out.
There is the newspaper to retrieve,
delivered by some poor devil
who rises in darkness to make sure I have it
with morning coffee on the porch

near to her who arranges flowers in a vase
while I rock back and forth,
grandfather's clock ticking in my ear

—*Robert Riche*

## OPENING

I.
You must leave the narrow place
the chrysalis which confines.
You will know when the moment comes
encased in hope you will emerge

from the Red Sea, a path opens
and yes, you will see the broken chariots
of those who wanted you
to stay, confined and enclosed.

The towers of water on either side
will hold the path clear
but not for long.
You will wonder how you were so brave.

There will be song, buoyant and joyful
and others will guide you.
The first step leads to the next one after
like the chain from kiss to caress.

II.
Like the chain from kiss to caress
your lips travel across the map of my face
from my mouth to my ears
my neck.

Your hands travel across my body
over the down of my coat
and I want to say something
in your ear
but the words do not come
so I whisper breath
breathe into you.

Moon spills over the trees
blossoming, opening, radiating
The tulips about to emerge
will they be red or yellow?
or suncolored?

We are engulfed by opening.

(*continued*)

III.
We are engulfed by opening

The cherry blossoms emerge—

the delicate encasings

which protected for so long

fall away


There is no turning back

The sea has parted

all of the moments of my life

open

       *—Deborah Leipziger*

# BOOK REVIEWS
## by Doug Holder

**To the Dark Angels**
by Jared Smith
*New York Quarterly* Books

Jared Smith is a poet who has an intimate knowledge of the failure of language; yet he still writes, and writes powerfully. In his lead poem, "Shivering Between Beings," in his accomplished new collection, *To the Dark Angels*, he acknowledges this with poetic resignation and appreciation: "What we build endures / from the fleet-footed animals/grained grasses / spaces between stars / endures beyond understanding / white within darkness / in the primeval without words." This is a theme that reappears throughout the book. Smith, who has a great affinity for the working stiff, the "Hey, Joe what do you know?" everyday guy trying to make the daily nut, performs his work with words despite all their limitations. He punches in for the countless eight hour shifts, and puts in the hard work needed to convey beauty and truth.

Although many of the poems here are focused on nature (Smith now lives in the hills outside Denver), Smith was a resident of New York City when he first cut his teeth on the literary world, and knows how to capture the ethereal beauty of the cityscape. In his poem "Back Briefly to the City" he conveys the allure, the endless possibility platter, the dream New York offers. Here you have a picture of the poet pining for a drink, and meditating on a vision of a cab as it disappears into the mystery of the night: "That's why I've come here now, it seems, but I'd like a drink first / and to choose among the many sleek women in their furs with / all the secrets of taxi cabs run out into the city night on sequined feet."

Smith rails against the buzz, the byte, the incessant demands of the cell phone, the quick fix, and the fragments of conversation that transpire over a wireless world. To this poet, to create art is a slow and contemplative process:

> "... It takes raw youth
> and time to work the patterns, shape clay
> with colors carrying the patina of meaning
> a time that lingers between the workings
> of grandfather clocks and cell phones,
> accumulating in the dust of empty rooms.
> No instant messages, no quick network
> comes from this where time stands, still,
> just a slow communication that enfolds."

Smith wants to impart a message; he wants readers to take notice—before they send their next text or email, before they don their headphones—before they shut themselves off to the world.

## Dead Lions

by A.D. Winans

Punk Hostage Press

A.D. Winans, founder of the ground-breaking San Francisco-based *Second Coming Press* and doyen of the San Francisco poetry scene for the past 40 or 50 years, has published a new book of essays entitled *Dead Lions*. In these essays, Winans focuses on four writers: screenwriter Alvah Bessie, one of the Hollywood Ten who appeared in front of the House Un-American Activities Committee in the 1950s; Jack Micheline, the poet and Whitmanesque wanderer; Charles Bukowski, the dirty old man of poetry; and Bob Kaufman, one of the great Beat poets to come out of the North Beach scene in San Francisco.

Since I am primarily a poet, I am most interested in Winans' accounts of Micheline, Bukowski, and Kaufman. Winans aptly starts with Micheline's death on a San Francisco subway. A poetic death in transit, like Lowell's in the back of the cab. Winans recounts Micheline's wanderlust, his prolific trips across the country, and his outrageous behavior fueled by booze. Although Micheline published 20 books, he was spurned by the City Lights Press, Black Sparrow, and other notable publishers because of his "offensive" behavior. But Micheline never changed his ways. Winans writes:

> He refused to bow to anyone, choosing to write for the people, hookers, drug addicts, blue collar workers and the dispossessed, and he did it from deep inside the heart.

Micheline was befriended by Bukowski, but Bukowski did not share the religious fervor that Micheline brought to his poetry. Yet Bukowki still respected the man. Winans quotes from a letter Bukowski sent to him:

> Micheline is all right—he's one third bull shit, but he's got a special divinity and special strength. He's got  perhaps a little too much of a POET sign pasted to his forehead, but more often than not he says good things—in speech and poem—power-flame, laughing things. I like the way his poems flow and roll. His poems are total feelings beating their heads on barroom floors.

Much has been written about Charles Bukowski, and in fact Winans has written a memoir published by Dustbooks called *The Holy Grail: Charles Bukowski and The Second Coming*, which I reviewed years ago for the *Small Press Review*. Still, it is interesting to hear Winans' take on things again, in a different context. Winans met Bukowski when Winans was publishing his *Second Coming* magazine in San Francisco. He even had an issue dedicated to Bukowski. Winans sees many admirable qualities in the BUK—but he gives us the full view of this man with the pockmarked face:

> Hank was a man of many virtues, but to see him (as many do) as a man whose motive and actions were in the best interests of the down and out, simply ignores the fact he betrayed and tore apart many former friends, both in short stories and in vindictive poems, frequently breaking off friendships whenever someone got too close to him, and often on brutal terms.

Winans points out that besides his poetic acumen Bukowski was a great entertainer. Here, Winans describes Bukowski on stage, before his reading:

> Once on stage, he wasted no time in opening the refrigerator door and popping open a can of beer to the sound of wild cheers. I watched him survey the crowd for several seconds before tilting his head back and drinking half the contents from the beer can. Again this simple act was met with rousing cheers.

The North Beach section of San Francisco is now more of a tourist destination, as gentrification of the city has forced out many of the poets and writers because of astronomical rents. I recently saw some footage from a documentary with Lawrence Ferlinghetti, Founder of City Lights Books, who talked about the high tech sector coming in and gutting the city—to the point where he barely recognizes it. But in the 50s and 60s this was a hotbed of creative energy.

North Beach is a six block area in the city from lower Grant Avenue to upper Grant Avenue. Poet Bob Kaufman, known as the "American Rimbaud," was a prime player here. He co-edited the well-known lit mag *Beatitude* with William Margolis. Kaufman was the son of an Orthodox Jew and an African-American mother, and he was brought up in New Orleans. His best-known book was published by the noted avant-garde press, New Directions. The book, *Solitudes Crowded with Loneliness*, created quite a stir in the local literary community. Winans hung out with Kaufman in the Co-Existence Bagel Shop, a happening spot at the time and he recalls the very dramatic poet:

> Kaufman entered the establishment, climbing on top of the tables, and reciting a newly written poem…The audience hung on his every word.

Later Kaufman got into difficulty with the police and was often hauled to the city prison after he wrote on the walls of the bagel shop: "Adolf Hitler, growing tired of Eva Braun, and burning Jews, moved to San Francisco and became a cop."

The book is chock full of Winans' fly on the wall accounts of these renegade poets and writers. This is not a scholarly book; there is no intensive analysis of their work; but it is a lively introduction to these men—and well worth the read. The book should whet the readers' appetite and, one hopes, encourage them to explore these men further. I did find myself wondering about the women poets of this era—but perhaps that is a topic for another book.

## DOOLEY FOR STATE REP

A small band of supporters
holding up signs and waving
on the corner of Pleasant and Main
on this gelid November morning—and who
is Dooley? He's the one among them
who isn't wearing a hat, the one
with the gelled hair, very red
ears, frozen smile, waving at me
as I drive by, the wind chill
minus twenty, his breath sending out
these little diplomatic envoys
of wispy white warmth every which way.
This man without the hat, without
the sense to put on a hat in weather
like this, this man who wants my vote,
who wants to represent me in the capital,
this man who made the bad decision
to forgo the hat this morning because
it would cover his excellent hair,
or it would make him look weak
when he needs to look strong,
needs to look excellent, and I think
this is exactly what's wrong with America
and its leaders, and its image in the eyes
of the world: it all comes down to this
hat, which this man who wants my vote
but shall not have it, doesn't have on.

—*Paul Hostovsky*


## WEEKDAY MORNINGS

We had a copper kettle that nobody ever shined.
My father filled it to the brim on cold winter mornings.
His egg at the bottom, kettle boiled, egg cooked,
he made the tea and our mother's toast.

After the breakfast there was plenty of water left,
enough to wash and shave at the kitchen sink.
I see him now, in his vest, braces loose
shaving by a round mirror, his face white with soap,

unaware of the cold, or us as we sat alongside
eating porridge, the dog under the table, hopeful.
Our mother had her tea and toast in bed—
she hated the smell of eggs.

—*Triona McMorrow*

## TERSE PRAISE FOR X.J. KENNEDY*

Oh Kennedy, what caused your pen to stray?
Yes, what would William Carlos Williams say?
The pound of that stress, the wink of that rhyme,
Your wry charming muse set the paradigm.
Lost scribblers, you led them from pharaoh's waste
Of straw-less mud-poems, you poker-faced
Old pirate. You posed non compos mentis
To grim souls, plotted not a little fuss,
Then stood back to watch as gates imploded
With country-versed folk, each scene decoded.
Outlaws purloining metered craft soon proved
Your counter measures had begun, had moved
Those hidden relics from an ancient mound,
That melodic language once lost, now found.

*—Dennis Daly*

*This poem is a modest parody of X.J. Kennedy's
extraordinary "Terse Elegy for J.V. Cunningham."

## GARDEN OF THE LADYES

At midsummer, we sit together
in a cathedral of roses.
Jane Austin tells me stories about love and pride.
Charlotte keeps her secrets, her view soft as butter
and proud Titania dances with the fairies, as if in a dream.
The Dark Lady sings sonnets of lavender and foxgloves.
Wise Portia instructs me, all dark pink word,
masquerading in rosemary,
while fair Bianca's kiss tastes of snowy white myrrh.
Tamora, Queen of Goths whispers to pretty Jessica
and sweet Juliet flits here and there, wherefore art thou Juliet?
At midsummer, we sit together among the sage and thyme,
reciting verse in a cathedral of fragrance,
caressing poetry as if it were a rose in an English country garden.

*—Louisa Clerici*

## ON TURNING 60 IN EARLY SPRING

The pussy willows in a clear
blue vase after days send out roots

in the water—white strands as straight
as the stalks, where climb, inch

over inch, one side then the other,
buds of silvery fur.

Most buds plump and lengthen,
like fuzzy caterpillars

stretching from the branch.
Dark pores dot these buds

and send out white filaments
tipped with pollen dust.

While from within, the gray buds
are greening, out of the bark

the pale stems start—pushing
leaflets left and right,

their top side soft with down
and pearly in the sun.

Root me in such water
to grow in my silver time.

—*Gayle Roby*

## LATE SUMMER IMPROV

On grounds of old estate
breezes play melodies
in aged trees during
gaps in concert; take
advantage of each delay.
The improvisation moves
in fathomless directions;
some playful, some dark,
some drop us into an abyss
of endless reverie.
Sun's footprints tread lawn,
directions for a fanciful dance.
Seals broken; corks lifted;
wine poured over ice
on this sultry afternoon.
A few cows wander by;
an occasional leaf lands
lightly on the grass.
Evils of the world
forgotten in this moment
of transitory bliss.

—*Lainie Senechal*

## ONE LIFETIME, AMONG MANY

Though it was the Venus of our tongues
that awoke revelation,
the honesty of our bodies sparked an epic arc,

and I have spent years trying to decipher the rhyme,
years wondering how many centuries ago we were bonded,
wondering how long our strophes have interplayed;

how long, I ask,
has your cadence been the lilt
beneath my lines?

We were ancient poets; we must have been;
poets struck by the mysticism in the constellations,
our pens spilling lore; we watched over men,
writing out the stories of the stars.

You, my love, were just and bright;
I was gentle; I was seductive.

I am as fond of seduction as you are of your scales;

still, I could rage and you would water me with your laugh,
ever the balance to my fire,
but you knew then, and now,
how to keep the embers of my heart glowing.

In this lifetime, we have found ourselves
separated and practical,
logical and tamed,
when once we were free to be wild;

but we have not forgotten,
and we have not changed, your heart ever fair,
my hair long enough
to veil navel and breast.

—*Rene Schwiesow*

## THE LITTLE RAT, THE FLOWER
## OF THE GUTTER

*Dance is poetry with*
*arms and legs. It is*
*matter, gracious*
*and terrible, animated,*
*embellished by movement.*

Marie could never have spoken those
words, only uttered them with her body,
a language pulling Degas in seductively,
intensely. He saw the dancers, especially
Marie, luring him, offering him a display
in which he could find certain human
secrets. Dancers as martyrs, their ability
to endure, exhausted, starved. Some
dark insistence, tangled, dusty. An ebony
shadow maybe around an elbow, a
heel, an armpit, the nape of a neck, a
calf muscle. The image goes dark and has
nothing to do with any shadow. The
darknesses express the pain of endurance,
what a ballet critic said, "Baudelaire called
gracious and terrible." The
air of dancing, the air of a dancer's
entire wracked body to become
one with the music, Degas managed
to capture this experience
silently

—Lynn Lifshin

## JOLIE-LAIDE

*Not pretty or ugly but a*
*look that not only combines*
*attributes of both but suggests*
*a deeper sense of conflict between*
*appearance and inner life.*

The little dancer,
Degas' little rat
from the slums of Paris.
Fascinated by the street
urchin, Degas wrote a sonnet
about such a girl, that she
might have a good life
without losing the "race of
the street." Unlike white
marble, something to
admire, brown wax invited
something to be studied,
dissected and penetrated, in
all its implications. Surly,
a mix of arrogance and fear
the little dancer, mysterious
and somehow challenging
men to fantasize that
whatever they do to her body
they can't have or know her.

—Lynn Lifshin

## CRAWLING STONES

He was an insensitive bastard, with his
heart a stone, his eyes, a stone, his legs, a stone,
his arms, a stone
Crawling stones reaching

I got scratched, an achy body, every time
I was with him.

Once in awhile, I would take one of his stones and
throw it across the river, watching it hop across
the water, sinking…

One gone, many more to go.
One by one, in the water, to the bottom
of the river bed.

He finally drowned and me, I soared
like a bird, flying across the water, singing.

—*Gloria Mindock*


## BROKEN LOVE

Their first legitimate child was a girl—
a punishment, for giving up the boy
to strangers? A baby, making their world
complete; why then, did life seem to lack joy?
They went through the gestures of family:
small dresses washed, hair brushed, and put in braids,
pats on that tidy head—but who was she,
neither first-born, nor heir? The price they paid
for sin! Three daughters more, never another son.
They searched for their boy, left so long ago
in the old neighborhood. There was not one
trace to be found, as if they had borne no
son at all. Mourning the child that they lost
absorbed them. Their four daughters paid the cost.

—*Denise Provost*

# THE INVEIGLEMENT OF LIGHT

Cosmologists say starlight is old news
no matter how swiftly it flies.
From it we can only discern what was.
Leaves us humans behind the times.

For all we know at any given moment
every star in the sky has disappeared
gone on holiday
elsewhere.

A minute ago our sun
may have joined them,
yet it's light will shine somewhere on Earth
at least seven minutes more.

However we devise to peer and squint
at ancient light to try and scry the future from the past
we are consigned to live estranged by time
if this be our only guide.

Quantumists can't imagine how or why
but something travels faster still than light.
Mystics know all that we are, this stuff of stars
is woven into real time into the connected Whole.

—*Laura Senechal*


## LAST FLIGHT

*For Ronnie Sidner*

Most humans, in their earthbound minds,
think the beings that carry their souls aloft
are angels—white-robed and man-shaped with feathered wings.
But we were your honor guard, the bats you loved—
furry brown and rodent-shaped with wings of skin
stretched delicately over lengthened finger bones,
yet swifter and more agile than those angels,
sweeping, soaring, wheeling in our clouds of bodies,
ranks aligned with wind and terrain seen with echoed sound.
You saw our beauty, and we saw yours.
You we carried, at last joined with us in flight,
free of earth's anchor as we can be.
Now someone else must count us from below.

—*Keith Tornheim*

## TWO BEGINNINGS IN BOSTON

Michael came out half-baked
and finished up in the incubator.
It took him a week to learn to suckle.
We spent hours each day in the NICU
kangaroo-ing him next to our skin
and learning CPR before we took him home.
I worried so much over everything I did for him.
At six weeks I worried he'd not yet smiled,
then realized he had no role model for smiling.

The nurse was frantically calling for a doctor
when Celia was born,
but she managed to break out on her own.
As she was being cleaned up across the room,
I summoned myself to address her:
*Hi, Sweetie.  I'm right here.*
She turned her head straight to me,
strong-willed and ready, she basked
in the love first forged by her brother.

*—Linda Haviland Conte*


## DIRECTIONS TO WENDY AND POLLY'S PARADISE ON LOAN

Take off your watch. The trip takes as much time
as it takes. Let go of expectations.
It will rain, it will sun, it will thunder,
it will do whatever it likes, and you will
love it. Traffic, tolls, the red pick-up truck
tailgating—none of that matters.

When you turn off the interstate, try
to drive behind a horse trailer for the fourteen
miles, something to slow you down,
get you ready for the pace. Steer through
Andy's parking lot to the gravel lane ahead.
On the green fence, the brass number shines.

Pull right into the driveway. The lake
will be in front of you, ready to
embrace. But first, the house—full
of light, breezes, their memories, and
their love—waits for you. Enter.
Time to make memories of your own.

*—Susan Lloyd McGarry*

## THE REELING

I don't usually talk with strangers on the train, but something
about you reminds me of my father fishing off the pier,
pulling in his line to check everyone else's luck, content
to snag conversations here and there, while my brothers
and I cast our hooks and worms into the breezy lake.

You tell me you're disgusted with the children of Ted Williams.
Ted, who wanted only to be sprinkled over the warm blue waters
of the Gulf of Mexico, lies frozen, as his children argue over his money
and his genes. I tell you my husband wants to know if the son thinks
his dad's DNA is worth so much, how come *he's* not a famous ballplayer.

And you say, well, you knew Ted, you were in the Navy together,
a good guy, a real hotdog flying missions, who'd think nothing
of standing everyone at the bar. Strangely, I can say I have a connection
too, to both Ted and his children. My neighbor Florence, who once lived
in my old apartment in Watertown, used to babysit for them there.

So, Ted and his children were in my very kitchen, years before I was,
eating Florence's pressed pizzelle, though she's passed away now, too.
Then you reach a hand to your heart, drawing out a photo of a smiling woman
in a green dress, your wife, you say, gone ten years, today. And you open up,
like a layered box filled with feathered lures, bobbers and weights, hard shining

memories of her—the whirlwind romance, how you flew to South America
to learn her language. A doctor in Chile, she settled for nursing in the States
to be with you. After twenty good years together, it was you who nursed her
at the end. I dread my father leaving, already so much of him gone to me.
The dead always dying, we must talk them off the piers, all of us casting about.

—*Mary Buchinger*

## THIS MAN IS ASLEEP

This man is asleep
and in his sleep
he is more closed
than most people are
when awake.
How is this possible?
the vulnerable softening
of the body,
the deep drowning sleep,
his damp breathing
floating him further
into a dark cave
whose walls are crystal.
His arms around me loosen.
Earlier we are together,
now he is in his chestnut
kernel, spiky.
This man is asleep
around his own
heart, a geode
whose outside is granite
and impermeable. Perhaps
he is dreaming
of sharp crystals somewhere
of ripe secrets, of a
narrow beam of light
or of the one
firm tap
that would uncrack him
utterly, falling open
exposed, in his gleaming
jewelry, perfectly halved.

—*Kathleen Spivack*

## GOLF OUTING

the river runs through it and
the Vesper is the premier club
in greater Lowell
judges and lawyers and
bail bondsmen golf there
but just like the Vesper
the Tyngsboro Country Club
is on the Merrimack River too
and it was the TCC
for my bachelor party
Jimmy is my little brother
he's six four and weighs 295 pounds
my bigger brother Mark
says Jimmy's just
a thought of a veal cutlet
away from three hundred
  the bachelors' party outing was small
the two dads and me first and then
my two brothers and brother-in-law to be
my brothers care nothing about golf
they were drinking right away
and they didn't get along with Hugo
both my brothers were hockey players
they would run up to the ball on its tee
and shoot it like it was a puck
and really it'd go pretty long
well by the eight ball
Hugo my future brother by marriage
had had it
walks up to us old guys
and asks can I play with you guys
your brothers are going
to throw me into the river
and I look behind
and both my brothers
are chanting Bruno Bruno
with Jimmy is doing swimming gestures
and Mark both hands in front of him
like he's praying but then
he goes into a fake diving motion
as if into a pool or ocean or maybe a river

—*Michael Casey*

## REST STOP, TAMPA BAY

De Soto made landfall more or less right here
where the tourists let loose the dogs
along this curtailed patch of beach,
south of the Sunshine Skyway Bridge.

A desolate, abandoned village met
De Soto when he made landfall here.
We find a fist-sized conglomerate rock
along this curtailed patch of beach.

Striated imprints of twenty thumbnail shells,
abandoned homes of desiccated scallops, met
by mud and eons' complacent pressure.
A fist-sized conglomerate rock

with mud-brown ghost of trilobite pressed underside.
Striated imprints of twenty thumbnail shells:
limestone chalk highlights the banded arcs.
Out of mud and eons' complacent pressure

this grey stone matter appears to eye and hand.
With mud-brown trilobite pressed to the palm
it cups securely in my grasp.
Limestone chalk brightens banded arcs,

hairs'-width brushstrokes across a blunted wedge.
Grey stone matter appears to eye and hand
a tool to strike, a fragment to split.
It cups securely in the grasp,

thumb, index, middle fingers clasp
shell impressions edging this blunted wedge.
I think this had been chiseled out, hewn as
a tool to strike, a rock fragment to split

oysters. Along this curtailed patch of beach
thumb, index, middle fingers clasp
a fantasized prehistoric souvenir. I want to
think this had been chiseled out, hewn

and left behind long before De Soto, dropped
among the oyster shells. This patch of beach
features a dog named Charlie, snuffling toward us
and our wishful prehistoric souvenir.

South of the Sunshine Skyway Bridge,
a patch of beach where the dogs let loose,
a village found abandoned at De Soto's landfall,
more or less right here.

—David P. Miller

## THE PRELIMINARY ROUNDS

As your son's teacher, I'm supposed to tell you something
about his development in school,
his understanding of Ancient History,

but I don't know what to say exactly,
except the obvious: the rope has slipped his grasp
and his boat has drifted back into that soft fog of adolescence.

He began the semester with a soupcon of interest—
taken by Hannibal, and those militant elephants stumbling
across the Alps and Pyrenees in the Second Punic War,

but by test time he quietly faded away,
as if his interest were drawn in chalk,
and nothing we did or said reignited that spark.

I don't know, maybe he'd be better off
playing his guitar until his fingers ache beyond sore,
chord by homemade chord, swim in his own art

late into the night and come to the study of history—
and all that history reveals about our impulses, our violence,
our frailty, our intermittent brilliance—in his own time.

Or perhaps this class is too stifling—dulled, as it is,
by the need for order and pace, by the hammering of "rigor."
Perhaps he would open up if we took to the fields more,

or the mountains and lakes, or the lovely indifferent shore.
There, maybe, he'd be our leader, first to find sharks' teeth
among the stones and shattered, sea-worn shells,

pose questions fueled by unguarded enthusiasm for life.
Not that we venture out like that in this course. I'm just saying,
you never know with kids. That's the maddening part.

You fall in love with a young man's mind, praise him
with straight A's, and twenty years later he's drinking too much,
starting his third marriage and his fourth job in corporate sales.

It's the ones who hum along in their own dreams,
who intuitively know how to get by, like runners
surviving the preliminary rounds to make the finals—

they're the ones who burst forth one day, publish a book,
land a role on Broadway, establish some small quirky company

that blooms overnight into the darling of Wall Street.

But it doesn't always work that way, either.
Sometimes the ones who sail through keep on sailing—
good grades, good jobs, loving spouses, brilliant children,

content Saturday afternoons in the garden of good fortune,
no curse or cancer surfacing anywhere.
And sometimes the slackers stay slack.

They don't care now and they won't care later.
What happens is what happens. Time is time.
Love is to take or leave, or take and take.

So what does this say about the teaching profession?
Despite all the cajoling, pop quizzes, free pencils, the truth is
I don't know the first thing about your son. Do you?

Maybe the transparency of our own uncertainty
has left him stupefied. Maybe he already knows
what he wants to be when he awakens to the searing

knowledge of impermanence. Maybe he's waiting
for fate to trigger any sort of something. Maybe
he's already there, patiently waiting for us to catch up.

                                        —*Michael Brosnan*


## IS THIS LIKE WAITING FOR GODOT?

Waiting for the bookshelves

That may never come—

And the books in storage
Waiting for a congenial place

To rest, actually call home.
I realize the universe

Does not consider this to be
Of overriding importance—

But the universe is often lost
like a character outside Paramus.

Waiting for the bookshelves…

                                        —*Tim Suermondt*

## WAITER, THERE'S AN ELEPHANT IN MY SOUP

You call the waiter, who examines, then shakes his head:
"No, no, that's just a piece of watercress and it belongs there."
But you're not convinced. You pick it up in your soupspoon,
where it taps its right front foot as if testing the water. "Yes,
yes," the waiter says. "Let me get you a fresh bowl." "Look,"
you direct the waiter. "Real tusks."
"Yes, yes," he says.

You can't let it go. A living creature  flushed down the drain?
Take it home and keep it in a cage? Make a shtick of it:
Sell tickets to the neighbors, go on TV? Become maybe
a celebrity, fielding questions to which you have no answers?
The waiter can't help you, and when he takes away the bowl,
you keep the elephant on your spoon. When your entrée
comes you carefully put the elephant in the salad,
where he grazes placidly.

You pay your check and wrap the creature carefully in a napkin,
and a little salad with him. Your lunch break's over now,
but you call the boss: you're sick and can't get to work today.
At home, your wife's on the phone and the children (Dr. King Day,
no school) are engrossed in savage interactive video games.
Nobody looks up, even when you show them the unwrapped
elephant on the spoon.

You think the elephant loves you. You read it in those big, deep eyes.
So, all celebrity dreams or even amusing the family are out the window.
You build a little cage that also fits the pocket. Sometimes you dream
that if the elephant should die you'd take up scrimshaw. But mostly
you have no secondary schemes. It's all about the elephant
and the infinite peace it gives you.

*—Bert Stern*

## IN A SPOT

If you were a bathroom, where would you be?
Such a peculiar form of inquiry!
Still, I attest that query was rendered verbatim.
It is an arresting thought, a question that would stop
That train in the middle of a span.

Were I to venture an answer, I might reply,
Turn left, down the hall from the throne room
At Buckingham Palace. Or, perhaps you might find
The loo if you turn right past the servants' quarters
In a mansion facing the moors; or seek le petit cabinet
As you pass the Masters' Exhibit on a Saturday at the Louvre.
The MOMA's docent may direct you; the MFA's security, for sure.
Any place like a swank hotel offers opportunity for relief
And release from worldly stress.

If I were a water closet, I would not want to be
An outhouse in Winter's Northern Kingdom;
Nor would I wish to be a powder room
In a solitary lighthouse in the North Sea.
Nor would I want to be such a room of solitude
In the Moroccan Sahara; besides, it might only be a mirage,
A tough spot, to be in, if nature calls.
If I were in that plight, I might not answer at all.

I'm not sure what other folks do, safe and secure
Ensconced upon the throne behind locked doors
Of their comfort rooms. Perhaps they clip coupons
Or check their stocks. Maybe they tend to the business
Of washing sweat-soaked socks;
Or texting friends; posting on face book.

Libraries often find their way to the loo.
It's not my business what others may do.
As for me, I contemplate mortality;
What inspirations, I shall not tell
But, hidden away from a hard day's knocks,
I sense that it robustly surpasses
Plucking lint from my navel.

—*Harris Gardner*

## HE WOULD NOT STAY

Our cat would not stay at our new address.
New carpeting was foul to him, the shiver
Of bright lamps too strange. Far from the river
Now, he missed the routine restlessness

And we missed it too, how we missed the way
We lived our lives there, above the noise
And dogs, the Friday nights that vagrant boys
Got drunk and cursed our nascent dreams away,

Dreams that in the new place we'd have to hone
And shape and polish, work much harder at,
Enough to shake up our big sleepy cat,
Who chose to walk the distances alone

To conquer space; to leave, with every climb,
The present for the past and conquer time.

*—Joyce Wilson*


## STUNTMAN

Did you ever imagine your life ending like this,
Ju Kun? in a fall more fantastic than any you took

as the stuntman in Forbidden Kingdom—
this time for real, on your way home to China

to your wife and young sons, your flight
off course, plummeting into the Indian Ocean,

sinking into a seabed so deep and rugged
no one has found a sign of you yet—

sonar pings missing their mark,
your body unclaimed for mourning.

I picture your plane at the bottom of the ravine,
miles below the plateau near Broken Ridge.

You kick out a window, swim free
of the fuselage, doing somersaults, diving

among branched corals, frilly white sponges,
purple and yellow crinoids like stars.

*—Ruth Smullin*

## DRAGON FLY

I was cycling down from Belmont Hill
onto the marsh flats of Beaver Brook
when I saw the Green Darner
flipped and dancing on the road.
It was missing two right legs
but the arms still crooked
under the mosquito-devouring jaws.
If its magic had been as strong as its will
it would have soared into the blacktop
that had carried its destruction.

I marveled at my luck
to examine such a flyer close and so alive;
the needle body heaving
the six inch span of trembling cellophanes
the space-goggle eyes that tracked me;
once it had hunted with a precision
that mocked the computer-guided vanities
of Air-Force Phantoms.

It calmed in the cradle of my hand
and seemed to take comfort
in my attention to its beauty;
until, tugged by my journey,
I thought of euthanasia,
thought I would be kind and crush it,
because it would never again be
a wild hunter over the marshes.

Then, as if it had heard my thought,
the injured Darner tumbled from my hand,
righted itself,
                hesitated,
                        soared
and vanished in the background of the trees.

—*Wendell Smith*

*NOTE: The following two poems from the previous issue are being reprinted with corrections:*

### MUD FEAST
*For H.G.*

The fever raged and ate his name,
this bard on a Quest in the pitch of night.
The ground erased his sodden sense
of step by step slogging along it,
assuring him he wasn't sure at all.
He sought some edge of the edgeless plot
he must create now for the sake of waking,
for white moths by the millions made him shiver.
How he had come to this nowhere from nowhere
discernible, seemed ample cause to weep
or laugh, to bark or mutter oaths,
or even gather footnotes for the dense rant
he would compose, once he'd composed himself.
He'd risen an inch, a foot, perhaps a yard
above the rain-bombed path that snaked the woods.
He walked on air, though only mud made sense,
the sluck and slosh of gravitas such thoughts
as he'd be testing now, if he weren't dreaming,
and if the thousand questions posed him slyly
by shrewd and wakeful beings of the wood
did not instill in him to crave mud more
than any makeshift, dreamtime scroll of air
around his feet. He only had to get there
before they'd know he had no way of knowing
where he was going, though he'd heard the drums.
The feast they'd laid to celebrate his coming
was covered with bright laurel, till he'd come.

*—Tomas O'Leary*

## WINTER'S SPARROW

A small sparrow huddles
under the long bough
that leans, as if whispering a secret
to the frozen pond.

Blue smudges of lichen
mottle the tree bark, dark
against white-winter hush.
Unforgiving wind beats
the sparrow's ruffled coat.

She trembles in red-twig brush,
her rust-hued beak
folded under auburn down,
in search of spring's flush,
the smoke-white feathers
of her puffed belly, shivering.

Delicate claws clutch
a bare branch,
russet leaves still lingering
under a thin veil of rime.

A low wan sun
casts the darker shadows—
perhaps she has seen them.

With nature's patience,
she waits for verdant times.

*—Ruth C. Chad*

**Nina Rubinstein Alonso**'s poetry has appeared in *Ploughshares, The New Yorker, Bagel Bards, Ibbetson Street, The New Boston Review, MomEgg, U. Mass. Review,*etc., and her stories in *Southern Women's Review* and *Broadkill Review,* one a Pushcart nominee. David Godine Press published her book *This Body.* She works with Constellations a Journal of Poetry and Fiction (www.constellations-lit.com) and directs Fresh Pond Ballet School in Cambridge, Massachusetts (www.freshpondballet.com).

**Jennifer Barber** is the author of *Given Away, Rigging the Wind,* and *Vendaval.* She teaches in the English Department at Suffolk University in Boston, where she also edits the literary journal *Salamander,* now in its twenty-third year. Her recent poems have appeared in *Poetry* and *Pangyrus,* and this year she completed a translation of *Ici en exil* by French poet Emmanuel Merle. Translations from the book are forthcoming in the *Massachusetts Review, Metamorphoses, Modern Poetry in Translation,* and *Upstreet.*

**Molly Mattfield Bennett** has published in several magazines including *Knock, Antioch* (Seattle), and with the Bagel Bards. In 2010, *Name the Glory* was published by Wilderness House Press, and in June 2012 she was one of three poets to read at the Jeff Male Memorial Reading at the William Joiner Center Writers' Conference, University of Massachusetts, Boston. She has completed a new book, *Point-No-Point.*

**Michael Brosnan**'s poetry has appeared in various literary journals, including *Confrontation, Borderlands, Prairie Schooner, Barrow Street, New Letters,* and *Ibbetson Street.* He is the editor of *Independent School,* an award-winning quarterly magazine on precollegiate education. His book, *Against the Current: How One School Struggled and Succeeded with At-Risk Teens* (Heinemann), was the basis for the 2009 documentary film *Accelerating America.* He lives in Exeter, New Hampshire.

**Jessie Brown** has two short collections, *What We Don't Know We Know* (Finishing Line Press) and *Lucky* (Anabiosis Press). A resident of Arlington, Massachusetts, she leads poetry workshops for schools, libraries and community centers throughout the Boston area. In addition to publishing poems and translations in literary journals—such as *New Madrid, Comstock Review, Soundings East, American Poetry Review, Minerva Rising*—she collaborates on interdisciplinary projects with poetry and the visual arts. (www.JessieBrown.net)

**Mary Buchinger** is the author of *Aerialist* (Gold Wake, 2015; shortlisted for the May Swenson Poetry Award, the OSU Press/The Journal Wheeler Prize for Poetry and the Perugia Press Prize) and *Roomful of Sparrows* (Finishing Line). Her poems have appeared in *AGNI, Cortland Review, DIAGRAM, Fifth Wednesday, Nimrod International Journal of Prose and Poetry, The Massachusetts Review,* and elsewhere. She is Associate Professor of English and Communication Studies at MCPHS University in Boston, Mass.

**Michael Casey**'s first book, *Obscenities,* was in the Yale Younger Poet Series in 1972. Adastra Press published his latest book, *Check Points,* in 2014.

**Ruth C. Chad** Ruth Chad is a psychologist and poet, who lives and works in Newton, Massachusetts. Her chapbook, *The Sound of Angels,* is pending publication by Cervena Barva Press in 2015. She has published poems in *Montreal Poems, Lyrical Somerville, Ibbetson Street, Bagels with the Bards, The Aurorean* and The Psychoanalytic Couple and Family Institute of New England *Connection.*

**Louisa Clerici**'s stories and poetry have been published in literary anthologies and magazines including *Carolina Woman Magazine* and *The Istanbul Literary Review.* Louisa's poetry was chosen for the 2014 Mayor's Prose & Poetry Program commemorating the Boston Marathon tragedy. Her story, *The*

*Poet Moon*, is included in *Best New England Crime and Suspense Stories, 2015*. Louisa is a hypnotist and behavioral sleep coach at *Clear Mind Systems in Plymouth*, MA (www.clearmindsystem.net).

**Linda Haviland Conte** is currently working on a full-length collection of poems. She has received a grant from the Somerville Council for the Arts (2005) and a Cambridge Poetry Award (2003). Conte's chapbook *Slow As A Poem* was published by Ibbetson Street Press (2002). She works as a paraeducator in Somerville, Massachusetts, where she and her husband have just begun empty nesting.

**Robert Cording** is the Barrett Professor of creative writing at Holy Cross College; he has published seven collections of poems. A new book, *Only So Far*, is out this fall from CavanKerry Press.

**Dennis Daly** has published three books: *The Custom House* (Ibbetson Street, 2012), a verse translation of Sophocles' *Ajax* (Wilderness House, 2012), and *Night Walking with Nathaniel* (Dos Madres, 2014). Daly also writes reviews regularly for the Boston Area Small Press and Poetry Scene. Follow Daly's blog here: dennisfdaly@gmail.com.

**Beatriz Alba Del Rio** is a bilingual poet, lawyer, mediator, and member of the New England Poetry Club. Beatriz' awards include: 1st Prize, 2002 Octavio Paz International Poetry Contest; 3rd Prize, 2003 Pablo Neruda International Poetry Contest; 2004 1ST Prize, Cambridge Poetry Award ("*Masks Over Masks*" in the "female erotic poem" category, and finalist with "*Black Crows*" in the "female love poem" category); and 2007 3rd Prize, New England Poetry Club, Diana Der-Hovanessian Translation Award

**Brendan Galvin** is the author of seventeen collections of poems. Habitat: *New and Selected Poems 1965-2005* (LSU Press) was a finalist for the National Book Award. His crime novel, *Wash-a-shores*, is available on Amazon Kindle. *The Air's Accomplices*, a collection of new poems, is forthcoming from LSU Press in spring, 2015. Galvin lives in Truro, Massachusetts.

**Harris Gardner** has been published in *The Harvard Review, Midstream, Cool Plums, Rosebud, Fulcrum, Chest, Ibbetson Street, Main Street Rag, Facets, Vallum* (Canada), *Pemmican, WHL Review, Muddy River Poetry Review, Lummox,* and *Green Door*, and over 50 other publications. He was the poet-in-residence at Endicott College from 2002-2005; has been the poetry editor of *Ibbetson Street* since 2010; is the co-founder of Tapestry of Voices and the Boston National Poetry Month Festival (both with Lainie Senechal); and he has been a member of three Poet Laureate selection committees, two in Boston and one in Somerville.

**Adam M. Graaf** received his MFA from the University of Massachusetts Boston. He is an active member of Warrior Writers Boston where he facilitates writing workshops for veterans. Adam's work has appeared or is forthcoming in *War, Literature & the Arts, Breakwater Review*, and *CONSEQUENCE*. In 2013, he received the New England Poetry Club's The John Holmes Award.

**Lucy Holstedt** is a professor at Berklee College of Music and director of the Women Musicians Network. She serves on the board of the Boston National Poetry Month Festival, for which she produces an annual concert of poetry set to music and dance. Her poetry has been published in *Ibbetson Street* and several online and small press journals. Lucy lives in Somerville, MA with her husband—writer, artist and musician Kirk Etherton.

**Paul Hostovsky**'s latest book of poems is *The Bad Guys* (2015, FutureCycle Press). His poems have won a Pushcart Prize, two Best of the Net awards, and have been featured on *Poetry Daily, Verse Daily,* and *The Writer's Almanac*. He works in Boston as an ASL interpreter and Braille instructor. To read more of his work, visit him at www.paulhostovsky.com.

**Robert K. Johnson**, now retired, was a Professor of English at Suffolk University in Boston for many years. For eight years, he was also the Poetry Editor of *Ibbetson Street* magazine. His poems have been published individually in a wide variety of magazines and newspapers here and abroad. The most recent collections of his poetry are *Mist to Shadow, Flowering Weeds* and *Choir Of Day.*

**Adele Kenny**, founding director of the Carriage House Poetry Series, and poetry editor of *Tiferet Journal,* is the author of twenty-three books (poetry & nonfiction). Her poems have been published worldwide and have appeared in books and anthologies from Crown, Tuttle, Shambhala, and McGraw-Hill. She is the recipient of various awards, including NJ State Arts Council poetry fellowships, a Merton Poetry of the Sacred Award, the International Book Award for Poetry, and Kean University's Distinguished Alumni Award. She has read in the US, England, Ireland, and France, and has twice been a featured poet at the Geraldine R. Dodge Poetry Festival. (www.adelekenny.com)

**Alexander Levering Kern** is a poet, writer, and educator whose work appears in publications such as *About Place Journal, African American Review, Journal of the American Medical Association (JAMA), Caribbean Writer, Constellations, The Aurorean, Spiritus,* and *The Whirlwind Review* and anthologies from Ibbetson Street, Main Street Rag, and Pudding House. He is editor of *Becoming Fire: Spiritual Writing from Rising Generations* and serves as Executive Director of the Center for Spirituality, Dialogue and Service at Northeastern University in Boston. Alex lives in Somerville, Mass. with his wife Rebecca and children Elias and Ruthanna.

**Lawrence Kessenich** won the 2010 Strokestown International Poetry Prize. His poetry has been published in *Sewanee Review, Atlanta Review, Poetry Ireland Review,* and many other magazines. He has had three poems nominated for a Pushcart Prize. His chapbook *Strange News* was published by Pudding House Publications in 2008 and his full-length book *Before Whose Glory* was published in 2013 by FutureCycle Press and is available on Amazon.com.

**Valerie Lawson** has published in *Main Street Rag, BigCityLit, About Place Journal,* and others, with work forthcoming on *American Arts Quarterly*'s website. Lawson's first book, *Dog Watch,* was released in 2007. Lawson won awards for Best Narrative Poem and Spoken Word at the Cambridge Poetry Awards. She co-edits *Off the Coast* literary journal and teaches poetry at Sunrise Senior College at UMaine Machias. Lawson is a member of the board of the Maine Writers and Publishers Alliance.

**Deborah Leipziger** is an author, poet, and professor. Her chapbook, *Flower Map,* was published by Finishing Line Press (2013). In 2014, her poem "Written on Skin" was nominated for a Pushcart Prize. She is the co-founder of Soul-Lit, an on-line poetry magazine (http://soul-lit.com). Her poems have been featured in *Salamander, Ibbetson Street,* and the *Muddy River Poetry Review,* among other publications. Born in Brazil, Ms. Leipziger is the author of several books on human rights. To read her poetry, go to http://flowermap.net/

**Thomas Libby**, when writing in the 3rd person, is always surprised at just how little he has to say about himself. Originally from Portland, Maine, where everyone is a poet, he lives now with his wife and daughter somewhere between Boston and Providence, where he sometimes writes something down.

**Lyn Lifshin** has published over 130 books and chapbooks, including 3 from Black Sparrow Press: *Cold Comfort, Before It's Light* and *Another Woman Who Looks Like Me.* She also published *The Licorice Daughter: My Year With Ruffian* and *Barbaro: Beyond Brokenness.* Recent books include *Ballroom, All the Poets Who Have Touched Me, Living and Dead, All True, Especially The Lies, Light At the End: The Jesus Poems, Katrina, Mirrors, Persphone, Lost In The Fog, Knife Edge* & *Absinthe: The Tango Poems.* Also just out: *For the Roses,* poems after Joni Mitchell, *Hitchcock Hotel* from Danse Macabre and *The Marilyn Poems* from Rubber Boots Press. Her updated biography is also out: *Lips, Blues, Blue Lace: On*

*The Outside* as is a DVD of the documentary: *Lyn Lifshin: Not Made Of Glass.* (www.lynlifshin.com)

**Michael Gillan Maxwell** is a writer and visual artist in the Finger Lakes Region of New York State. Maxwell writes short fiction, poetry, songs, essays, lists, recipes and irate letters to his legislators. His work has been featured in a number of journals and anthologies. He served as associate flash fiction editor for *JMWW* quarterly journal and is currently editor of *MadHat's Drive-By Book Reviews*. A teller of tales and singer of songs, he's prone to random outbursts and may spontaneously combust or break into song at any moment. Maxwell can be found ranting and raving on his website: *Your Own Backyard* http://michaelgillianmaxwell.com.

**Susan Lloyd McGarry** is a freelance editor and former managing editor of the *Harvard Divinity Bulletin* (editing their 2012 poetry issue, *The Radiant Imagination)*. She has published poetry in several small magazines and gives readings and workshops. Named Bard of the 2004 Boston Irish Festival for her poem, "Memory of Coumeenole," she read there to more than 1000 people. Her poems have been anthologized in *The Poetry of Peace* and *Beyond Raised Voices*.

**Triona McMorrow** lives in Dunlaoghaire, County Dublin. She was shortlisted for the International Francis Ledwidge Poetry competition in 2009 and 2011. She was shortlisted for The Galway University Hospitals Arts Trust poetry competition in 2013. She has had poems published in *Ibbetson Street* journal in Boston, Massachusetts. In 2014, The Bealtaine group, of which she is a member, published an anthology of poetry titled *Bealtaine*.

**Gary Metras** is the author of *The Moon in the Pool*, Presa Press (April 2015) and the forthcoming *Captive in the Here* (Cervena Barva Press, summer 2015). His poems have appeared in *Ibbetson Street, The Common, Poetry, Poetry East,* and *Poetry Salzburg Review.* He lives in Easthampton, Massachusetts.

**David P. Miller**'s chapbook, *The Afterimages*, was published in 2014 by Červená Barva Press. His poems have appeared in publications including *Meat for Tea, Stone Soup Presents Fresh Broth,* the *2014 Bagel Bards Anthology, Muddy River Poetry Review, Wilderness House Literary Review, Oddball Magazine, Painters and Poets,* and the *Boston and Beyond Poetry Blog.* He has three "micro-chapbooks" available from the Origami Poems Project website.

**Gloria Mindock** is the founding editor of Cervena Barva Press, and one of the USA editors for *Levure Litteraire* (France). She is the author of *La Porţile Raiului, Nothing Divine Here,* and *Blood Soaked Dresses.* Widely published in the USA and abroad, her poetry has been translated into and published in Romanian, Serbian, Spanish, Estonian, and French. In December 2014, Gloria was awarded the Ibbetson Street Press Lifetime Achievement Award.

**Alfred Nicol** wrote lyrics for nine original compositions by classical/flamenco guitarist John Tavano. Their CD, released in January, 2015, is entitled *The Subtle Thread.* Nicol's collection of poetry, *Elegy for Everyone*, published in 2009, was chosen for the Anita Dorn Memorial Prize. His first collection, *Winter Light,* received the 2004 Richard Wilbur Award. His poems have appeared in *Poetry, Dark Horse, The Formalist, The Hopkins Review*, and other literary journals.

**Tomas O'Leary** is a poet, translator, musician, singer, artist and expressive therapist. He has published books of poetry: *Fool at the Funeral, The Devil Take a Crooked House*, and *A Prayer for Everyone*. His volume of new and selected poems, *In the Wellspring of the Ear,* will be out from Lynx House Press before spring's end. Meantime, he sings, plays his accordion and converses with wonderful people who have Alzheimer's.

**Miriam O'Neal** lives in Plymouth, Massachusetts with her husband and their dog (who doesn't know he is one, shhhhh). Her poetry and reviews have appeared in *Ragazine.cc*, *Marlboro Review*, *Blackbird Journal*, *The Guide Book*, and many other journals and magazines. She holds an MFA in Literature and Writing from Bennington College and teaches writing at University of Massachusetts, Dartmouth. Her current manuscript, *The World We Leave*, is looking for a home.

**Marilène Phipps-Kettlewell** is a poet, painter and short story writer. She has held fellowships at the Guggenheim Foundation, at Harvard's W.E.B. Du Bois Institute for Afro-American Research and the Center for the Study of World Religions, as well as at Radcliffe's Bunting Institute. Her collection, *The Company of Heaven: Stories from Haiti* won the 2010 Iowa Short Fiction Award, and is published by the University of Iowa Press. Her poetry won the Grolier Poetry Prize, while her collection *Crossroads and Unholy Water* won the Crab Orchard Poetry Prize and is published by Southern Illinois University Press. Her poems are also published in England by Carcanet Press and in numerous anthologies in the U.S. She is the editor of The Library of America's Jack Kerouac Collected Poems. Her website is at www.marilenephipps.com.

**Marge Piercy**'s18[th] poetry book, *The Hunger Moon: New & Selected Poems 1980-2010*, has been released in paperback by Knopf. Her newest collection, *Made in Detroit*, came out in March 2015. Piercy has published 17 novels, most recently *Sex Wars*. PM Press recently published her first collection of short stories, *The Cost of Lunch, Etc.* Her work has been translated into 19 languages and she has given readings, workshops or lectures at over 450 venues here and abroad.

**Denise Provost** has published in on-line and print journals, including Bagel Bards anthologies, *Ibbetson Street*, *Muddy River Poetry Review*, *qarrtsiluni*, *Quadrille*, *Poetry Porch's Sonnet Scroll*, and *Light Quarterly*. Provost lives in Somerville, Massachusetts, and currently studies with poet Susan Donnelly.

**Robert Riche** is the recipient of a National Endowment for the Arts grant, a Connecticut Foundation for the Arts grant, and an Advanced Drama Research grant, He has won the Stanley Drama Award, been a Breadloaf Writers Conference scholar and a Norman Mailer Writers Colony scholar. He has published one novel (published by The Permanent Press), two chapbooks, and two full-length poetry volumes, *Days Like These* and *In the Waiting Room*.

**Gayle Roby** received an MFA in Poetry from Warren Wilson College. Her work has appeared in several journals, including *The Iowa Review, The Ohio Review* and *Prairie Schooner*. She is a member of the Alewife Poets, and lives in Arlington, Massachusetts with her husband, son and cat.

**Rene Schwiesow** is co-host for the popular South Shore Poetry venue The Art of Words. Her publishing credits include *Muddy River Poetry Review, The Waterhouse Review, Ibbetson Street*, and *Midway Journal*. She is finalizing a poetry manuscript and the book will be forthcoming from Cervena Barva Press.

**J.D. Scrimgeour** has published two poetry collections, *The Last Miles* and *Territories.* With musician Philip Swanson he formed the performance group, Confluence (http://confluence-poetryandmusic.com) and released a CD of poetry and music, *Ogunquit & Other Works*. He lives in Salem, Massachusetts, where his ancestors were killed for being witches.

**Lainie Senechal,** poet, painter and environmentalist, has read and featured at many venues throughout New England. Her poetry has appeared in journals and anthologies including *The Aurorean, Ibbetson Street, Spare Change, Wilderness House Literary Review, The Larcom Review, The South Boston Literary Gazette, City of Poets.* She co-authored two volumes of poetry. Her recent chapbook is *Vocabulary of Awakening.* She was a winner in 2015 Eagle Festival Poetry Contest.

**Laura Senechal** lives in Tennessee where she tends gardens and chickens while keeping peace among her three cats. She pursues well-being on her way to discovering the purpose of her life. She rejoices in the divinity and healing of the natural world. Music and poetry are treasured companions on her journey.

**Zvi A. Sesling** is a prize winning poet. He edits *Muddy River Poetry Review,* publishes *Muddy River Books* and reviews for *Boston Small Press and Poetry Scene.* He is author of *King of the Jungle* (Ibbetson Street Press, 2010), *Across Stones of Bad Dreams* (Cervena Barva Press, 2011) and *Fire Tongue,* forthcoming from Cervena Barva Press. He lives in Brookline, Massachusetts with his wife Susan Dechter.

**Jared Smith** is the author of eleven volumes of poetry, including his just-released *To The Dark Angels* and his *Collected Poems: 1971-2011,* both from NYQ Books in New York. His poems, essays, and literary commentary have appeared in hundreds of journals in the U.S. and abroad over the past 45 years. He is on the board of *The New York Quarterly* Foundation, and is a contributing editor of *Turtle Island Quarterly.* He has also served on the editorial boards of *The New York Quarterly, Home Planet News, The Pedestal Magazine,* and *Trail & Timberline.* A former New Yorker, he lives in Colorado in the foothills of The Rockies.

**Wendell Smith** is a physician who lives in Melrose. His poetry has appeared in *Kansas Quarterly, Constellation, View Northwest* and elsewhere. He won the American Academy of Poets and Sidney Cox Prizes at Dartmouth College where he met Ramon Guthrie in the '60's. He hopes you will look into Guthrie's poetry because he thinks Guthrie's masterpiece *Maximum Security Ward* should become to 20th century poetry what Moby Dick became to 19th century fiction.

**Ruth Smullin** lives in the Boston area. Her poems have appeared in the Bagel Bards Anthologies, *Common Ground Review, Constellations, Crucible* (winner of the Sam Ragan Prize), *Ibbetson Street* #35 and #36, *Plainsongs,* and *Sow's Ear Poetry Review.*

**Laurie Soriano** is a poet and music attorney living in the Los Angeles area. Her book of poems entitled *Catalina* was published by Lummox Press in September 2011 and was named the Best Poetry Book of 2011 by the Independent Literary Awards. In 2012, her poem "Tree of Women" was nominated for a Pushcart Prize.

**Kathleen Spivack** is the author of nine books of prose and poetry, including the memoir *With Robert Lowell and His Circle: Plath, Sexton, Bishop, Kunitz & Others* and the prizewinning poetry book *A History of Yearning.* Her novel, *Unspeakable Things,* is forthcoming from Knopf. She teaches in Boston and Paris.

**Bert Stern**, at 85, has published two poetry collections, a critical study, a biography, and an environmental monograph that helped change Indiana's environmental regulations. His poems and essays have appeared in the *Anthology of Magazine Verse* & Yearbook American Poetry and in journals including *Poetry, American Poetry Review, Kenyon Review, New Republic, Southern Review,* and *China Daily.*

**Tim Suermondt** is the author of two full-length collections of poems: *Trying to Help the Elephant Man Dance* (The Backwaters Press, 2007) and *Just Beautiful* (New YorkQuarterly Books, 2010.) He has been published in many magazines and online, in places such as *Poetry, The Georgia Review, Prairie Schooner* and *Bellevue Literary Review* and has poems forthcoming soon in *Ploughshares, Plume Poetry Journal, Allegro Poetry Magazine* and *Blue Heron Review,* among others. He lives in Cambridge with his wife, the poet Pui Ying Wong.

**Keith Tornheim** is a biochemistry professor at Boston University School of Medicine. He was a co-winner of a Great Lakes College Association poetry contest in 1967 and is now a relapsed poet, with poems appearing in *Ibbetson Street, Poetica, Boston Literary Magazine, Muddy River Poetry Review* and *Lyrical Somerville (The Somerville News)*. His poems have been a part of High Holiday and other services of his congregation (see http://www.shirhadash-ma.org/poetry.html).

**Teisha Dawn Twomey** is the poetry editor at *Night Train*, as well as an associate fiction editor for Wilderness House Literary Press. She received her MFA in Poetry at Lesley University. Her poetry and short stories have appeared in numerous print and online poetry reviews and journals. By day, she is the Resource Specialist at Springfield College's Boston campus and, by night, she is (currently) at work on her first novel.

**Lee Varon** is a social worker and writer. Her work in adoption and foster care has been featured in *The Boston Globe, Boston Herald* and on *Lifetime Cable News.* In 2000, she published *Adopting On Your Own (Farrar, Straus & Giroux).* Her poems have been published in various places including *The Somerville Times* and *The Atlanta Review.*

**Joyce Wilson** is creator and editor of the Internet magazine *The Poetry Porch* (www.poetryporch.com), which has been online since 1997. Her poems have appeared, or will appear soon, in the literary journals *Alabama Literary Review, The Lyric, Gray Sparrow Journal,* and *Angle.* Her first book, *The Etymology of Spruce,* and a chapbook, *The Springhouse,* were published in 2010.

**A.D. Winans** is a native San Francisco poet and writer and the author of over 60 books and chapbooks of poetry and prose. He edited and published *Second Coming Magazine/Press* for 17 years. He is the recipient of a 2014 Kathy Acker poetry and publisher award, a 2006 PEN National Josephine Miles Award for excellence in Literature, and a 2009 PEN Oakland Lifetime Achievement Award.

**Amy Wright** is the Nonfiction Editor of Zone 3 Press and *Zone 3* journal and the author of four poetry chapbooks. She received a Peter Taylor fellowship for the Kenyon Review Writers Workshop, an Individual Artist's Fellowship from the Tennessee Arts Commission, and a VCCA fellowship. Her work appears in a number of journals, including *Brevity, DIAGRAM, The Kenyon Review, McSweeney's Internet Tendency,* and *Tupelo Quarterly.*